MACHINE TECHNOLOGY

Spinning Machines

Kay Davies and Wendy Oldfield

Titles in the series:

Cutting Machines

Digging Machines

Mixing Machines

Spinning Machines

Cover inset: Many toys and machines we use, such as a toy windmill and a bicycle, have spinning parts. Find out more about how a bicycle works on pages 12 – 13.

Title page: This operator is checking the threads on a spinning machine. Find out more about spinning machines on pages 22 – 3.

Series and book editor: Geraldine Purcell
Series designer: Helen White
Series consultant: Barbara Shepherd, (former) LEA adviser on the Design and Technology National Curriculum.
Photo stylist: Zoë Hargreaves

First published in 1995 by Wayland (Publishers) Limited
61 Western Road, Hove, East Sussex BN3 1JD, England.

© Copyright 1995 Wayland (Publishers) Limited

British Library Cataloguing in Publication Data
Davies, Kay
 Spinning Machines. – (Machine Technology Series)
 I. Title II. Oldfield, Wendy
 III. Bull, Peter IV. Series
 677.02852

ISBN 0 7502 1280 2
DTP design by White Design
Printed and bound by L.E.G.O. S.p.A., Vicenza, Italy.

Words in **bold** appear in the glossary on pages 30 – 31.

Contents

Tops and spinning

A spinning top, such as a humming top, will not balance unless it spins. It will not stop until it runs out of **energy**.▼

A cut-away view of the inside of a humming top

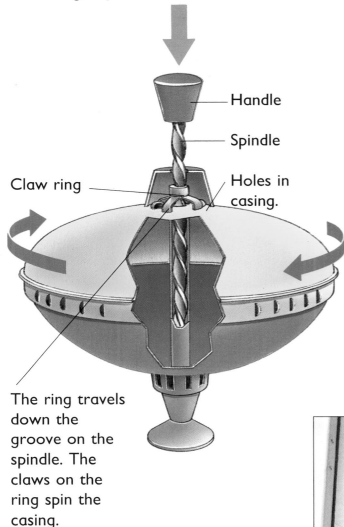

Handle

Spindle

Holes in casing.

Claw ring

The ring travels down the groove on the spindle. The claws on the ring spin the casing.

◀ A humming top has a metal **spindle** running through it. The handle is fixed to a rod with a spiral groove cut into it. When the rod is pushed down a ring with 'claws' on it fits into holes in the top's casing, or cover. The ring travels down the spindle's groove, which sets the top spinning. The rod only turns the spindle one way then it springs back.

A pump-handle screwdriver works in a similar way to a top. The rod inside the screwdriver can spin the **drill bit** both ways, to drive in screws or remove them. ▶

Wheel and axle

Wheels are used in many machines and tools to 'pass on energy'.

▼ The outer edge of a wheel, called the rim, turns around an **axle** at the wheel's centre. The rim of a wheel is bigger than its axle so the rim has to travel further when it turns.

When a wheel is used like a handle to turn an axle the smaller effort needed to turn the wheel creates more energy (or power) at the centre.

This energy is then 'passed on' to operate the next part of the machine or tool.

A steering wheel of a car is an example of a wheel and axle

The steering wheel is like a handle. Turning the wheel in a wide circle makes a stronger and tighter turn at the axle.

Axle

Steering wheel

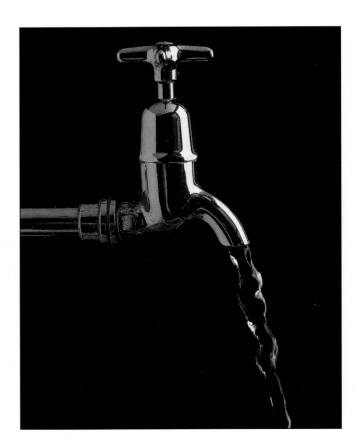

A cut-away view of the inside of a tap

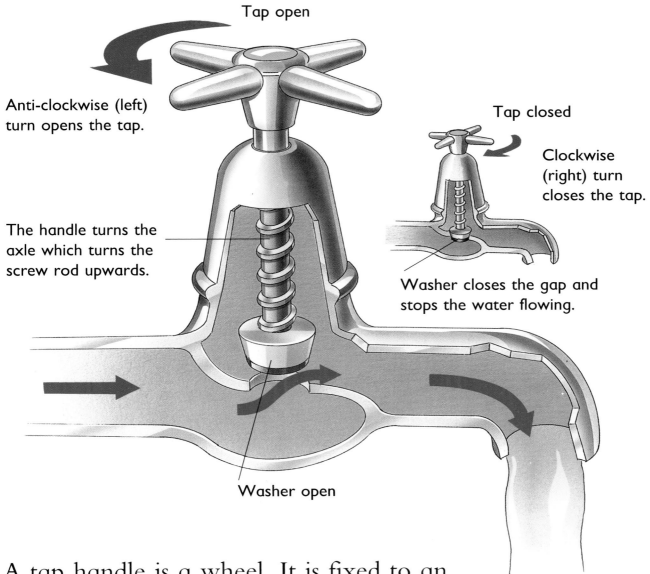

Tap open

Anti-clockwise (left)
turn opens the tap.

Tap closed

Clockwise
(right) turn
closes the tap.

The handle turns the
axle which turns the
screw rod upwards.

Washer closes the gap and
stops the water flowing.

Washer open

◀A tap handle is a wheel. It is fixed to an
axle that screws into the casing. When the
handle is turned anti-clockwise (to the left)
a rubber ring, called a washer, on the end
of the screw moves upwards. Water passes
through the gap. When the handle is
turned clockwise (to the right) the washer
closes the gap and the water stops flowing.

Drills

A spinning drill can make holes in wood, stone, concrete or metal. The end of the drill, called a bit, has a sharp cutting tip to **bore** into the material. Spiral grooves carry away waste.▼

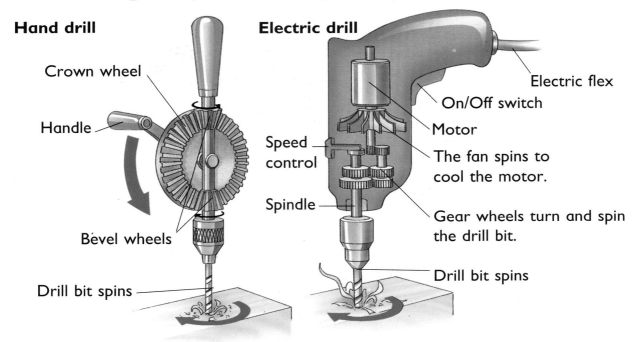

Hand drill

Crown wheel

Handle

Bevel wheels

Drill bit spins

Electric drill

Speed control

Spindle

Electric flex

On/Off switch

Motor

The fan spins to cool the motor.

Gear wheels turn and spin the drill bit.

Drill bit spins

▲Hand drills have **gear wheels** to spin the drill bit quickly. A handle turns a gear wheel, called a crown wheel, at the side of the drill. This spins two smaller **bevel** wheels as their teeth lock into the teeth on the crown wheel.

Because these bevel wheels are smaller than the crown wheel they turn more quickly. This spins the drill bit faster.

Electric drills are very powerful. A **motor** drives the gears inside. The gears turn and spin the drill bit. Electric drills have two sets of gear wheels for different speeds, slow and fast.▼

Spinning force

The inside of a salad spinner

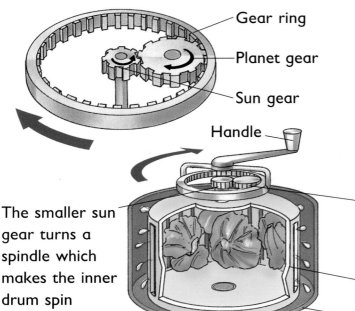

Gear ring

Planet gear

Sun gear

Handle

When an object is spun round in a circle it tries to fly out, in a straight line from the centre. This is called centrifugal force.

The smaller sun gear turns a spindle which makes the inner drum spin quickly.

When the handle turns, a gear ring moves which turns two smaller wheels, called a sun and planet gear, inside the ring.

Inner drum

Bowl

▲ A salad spinner uses centrifugal force to dry washed salad and vegetable leaves. The wet leaves are placed inside the inner drum which has slits in its side. The drum fits into a bowl with a handle on its lid. As the handle turns, the drum spins. The leaves stick to the drum's sides and the water is thrown out into the bowl.

A cut-away view of a washing machine

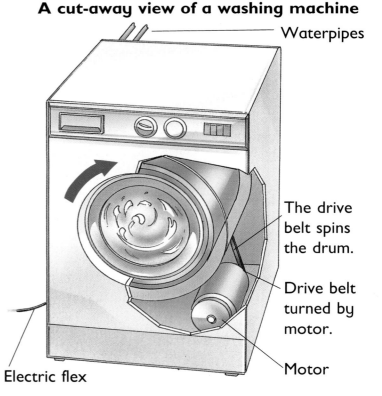

Waterpipes

The drive belt spins the drum.

Drive belt turned by motor.

Motor

Electric flex

10

▲ Washing machines and spin dryers also use centrifugal force.

A cut-away view of a spin dryer

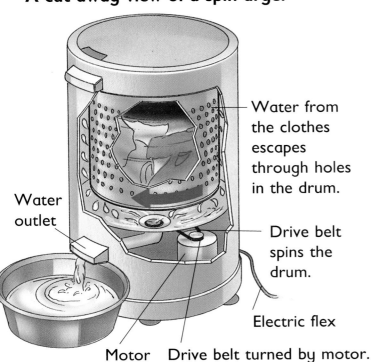

Water from the clothes escapes through holes in the drum.

Water outlet

Drive belt spins the drum.

Electric flex

Motor   Drive belt turned by motor.

◀ Wet clothes are put into the spin dryer's drum. As the drum spins, water from the clothes is thrown out through holes. Wet clothes are heavy so a lot of power is needed to spin them dry. To do this the spin dryer is operated by an electric motor. The motor turns a belt connected to the drum.

Chains going round

The pedals on a bicycle turn a large toothed wheel, called a sprocket. The teeth of this sprocket fit into gaps in a chain. As the sprocket turns so does the chain. The chain carries the spinning movement to smaller sprockets on the back wheel. These turn the wheel quicker than the pedals are turning. So, the energy used to turn the pedals is made into a greater **force** by the chain and sprockets.▼

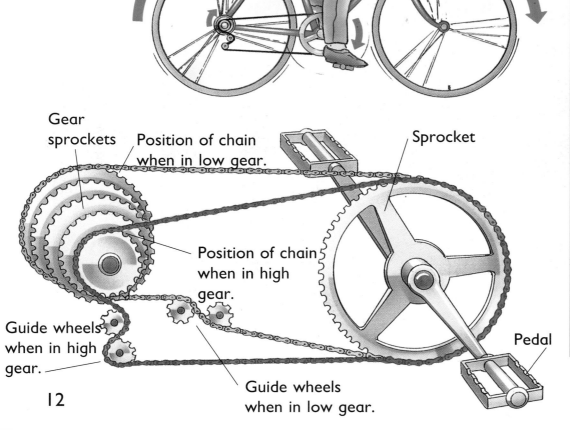

Gear sprockets

Position of chain when in low gear.

Sprocket

Position of chain when in high gear.

Guide wheels when in high gear.

Guide wheels when in low gear.

Pedal

Escalator

The stairs of an escalator are connected to a chain which **revolves** as it runs around a spinning **drive wheel**. This is turned by an electric motor at the top of the escalator. The weight of the returning stairs balances out the weight of the climbing stairs. All the motor has to lift is the extra weight of the people on the escalator.▼

A cut-away view of the inside of an escalator

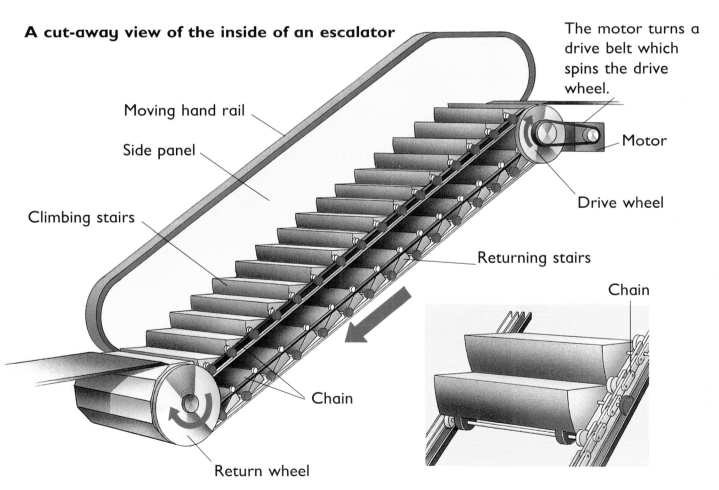

The motor turns a drive belt which spins the drive wheel.

Moving hand rail

Side panel

Climbing stairs

Motor

Drive wheel

Returning stairs

Chain

Chain

Return wheel

Clocks and watches

Mechanical clocks and watches have
many turning or spinning parts, such
as gear wheels. These gears connect
and move each other to measure
the time and work the hands on
the face.▼

When gears connect and work together it is called a gear train. This diagram shows the gear train inside a watch.▼

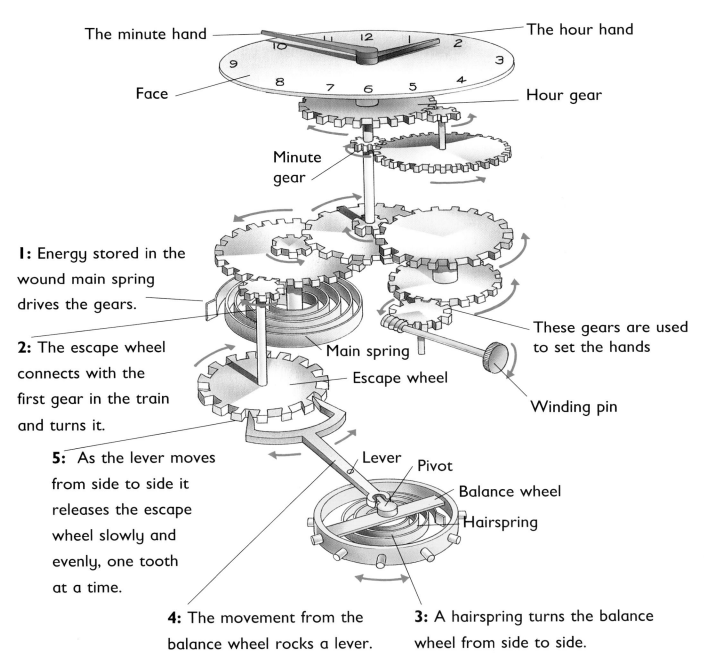

The minute hand

The hour hand

Face

Hour gear

Minute gear

1: Energy stored in the wound main spring drives the gears.

2: The escape wheel connects with the first gear in the train and turns it.

These gears are used to set the hands

Main spring

Escape wheel

Winding pin

5: As the lever moves from side to side it releases the escape wheel slowly and evenly, one tooth at a time.

Lever   Pivot

Balance wheel

Hairspring

4: The movement from the balance wheel rocks a lever.

3: A hairspring turns the balance wheel from side to side.

Wind power

Windmills were first used over a thousand years ago. They were used to grind grain (grass seeds) into flour or to drive a water pump.

The sails on a windmill spin when they catch the wind.

The sails act like a huge wheel. The power of the wind is turned into a greater force at the axle.

The axle turns a wheel, called the great spur wheel, which connects with gear wheels. The power is passed on by the gear wheels to turn the **grindstones**.▶

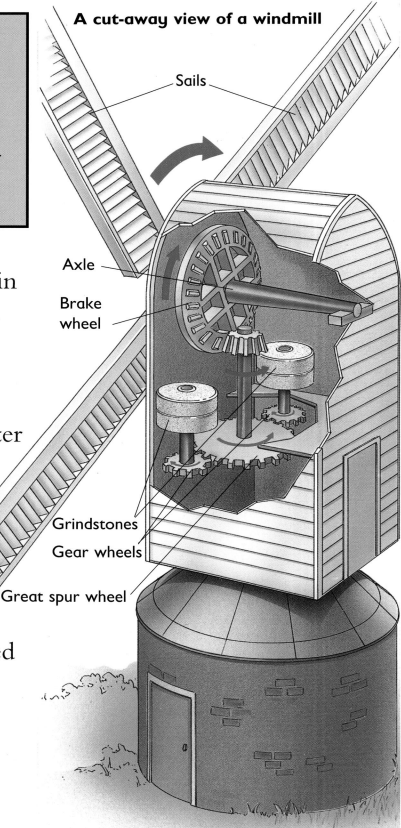

A cut-away view of a windmill

Sails

Axle

Brake wheel

Grindstones

Gear wheels

Great spur wheel

The inside of a wind turbine

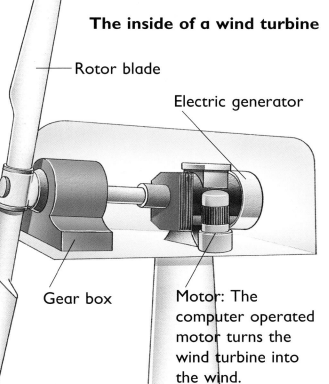

Rotor blade

Electric generator

Gear box

Motor: The computer operated motor turns the wind turbine into the wind.

▲ Wind **turbines** are a modern form of windmill. They drive a **generator** to make electricity.

The rotor blades can be up to 100 metres across. They are placed on concrete towers and are turned to face the wind by motors controlled by a computer.

Water power

Waterwheels were once the main way to produce power to work heavy machinery. The large waterwheel was fixed to the side of a mill.▼

Cut-away view of a waterwheel.

Sluice

Paddles

Axle

Water flowed through a **sluice** which controlled its flow. The water then poured on to the top of the waterwheel, or under it, to turn the **paddles**. The energy in the flowing water turned the wheel. This energy was then used to turn gears in the machines inside the mill. ▶

Water turbines have developed from waterwheels. They are contained in power stations at the bottom of large **dams**. Water flows through a sluice and down a tunnel. The water spins the turbine and turns the blades. The turbine drives a generator which can make enough electricity for thousands of homes.▼

Cross-section view of a water turbine in a dam

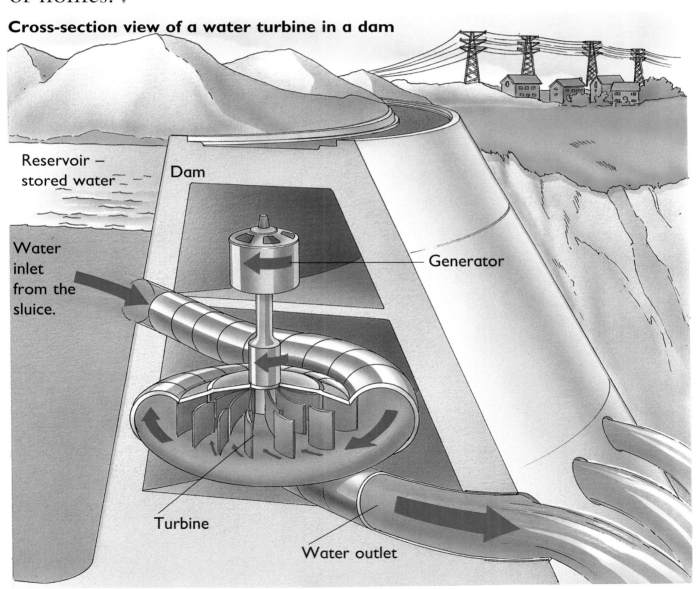

Reservoir – stored water

Dam

Water inlet from the sluice.

Generator

Turbine

Water outlet

Spinning yarn

Most natural fibres, such as wool and cotton, are short and weak. They have to be drawn out and twisted into yarn, or thread, before they are woven or knitted into cloth. This is called spinning.

Spinning yarn was once done by hand with a spinning wheel. ▶

A diagram to show how yarn is spun

1: The cleaned fibres are combed out straight by wire-toothed rollers.

2: They are then made into ropes called slivers.

3: Several slivers at once pass through a series of spinning rollers which stretch and twist them together into a 'roving'.

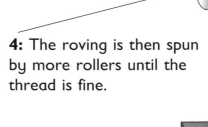

4: The roving is then spun by more rollers until the thread is fine.

In a modern spinning mill large machines are used to spin thousands of metres of yarn in minutes.

5: The finished yarn is wound on to bobbins.

Spinning machines can spin many lengths of yarn at once. The rollers are spinning all the time and the machinery is very noisy.▼

Moving pictures

Moving pictures in films trick our eyes and brain. A number of still pictures, or frames, pass in front of our eyes quickly each second. We keep the image of each picture in our brain until the next arrives. Each image comes so quickly that we think we see moving pictures.

Film cameras take twenty-four still pictures, or frames, every second. A spinning shutter separates each frame while the film is moved on. ▼

The inside of a film camera

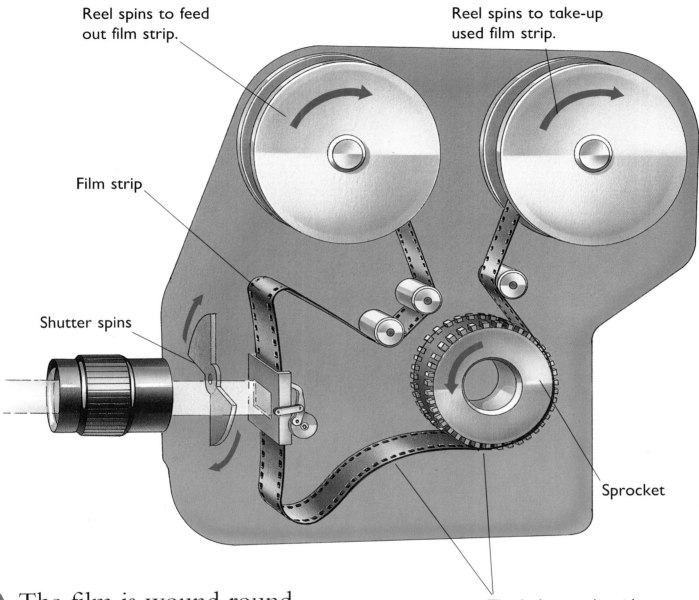

Reel spins to feed out film strip.

Reel spins to take-up used film strip.

Film strip

Shutter spins

Sprocket

The holes on the sides of the film strip connect with the teeth on the spinning sprocket wheel. This feeds the film through and on to the reel that takes up the film.

▲ The film is wound round the camera from one **reel** to the other by a sprocket wheel. The teeth on the sprocket fit into holes in the edge of the film.

Propellers

Hovercrafts can carry passengers and vehicles across water very smoothly because the craft floats on a cushion of air.

Hovercrafts are pushed along in the right direction by the action of spinning **propellers.** ▼

Turbine engines turn four propellers on a hovercraft. When the blades spin they lower the **air pressure** in front of them. This sucks the craft forwards. The spinning also forces air behind the propellers so the craft is also pushed forwards.▼

A cut-away view from the bow (front) of a hovercraft

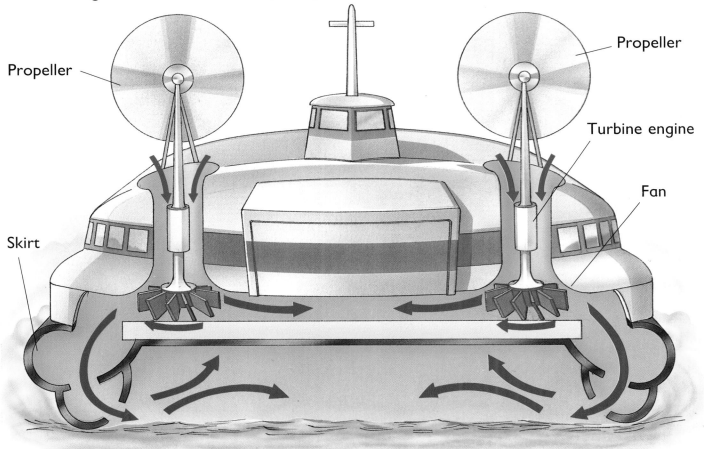

Propeller

Propeller

Turbine engine

Fan

Skirt

▲ The spinning turbine engines also power four large fans below deck. The fans blow air into a 'skirt'. This air-filled skirt lifts the hovercraft off the ground or water surface. This lets the hovercraft 'float' on top of the surface.

Spinning blades

▲ The spinning, curved rotor blades on a helicopter create 'lift'. This allows the aircraft to rise into the air and fly.

'Lift'
The upward force that keeps a plane or helicopter in the air.

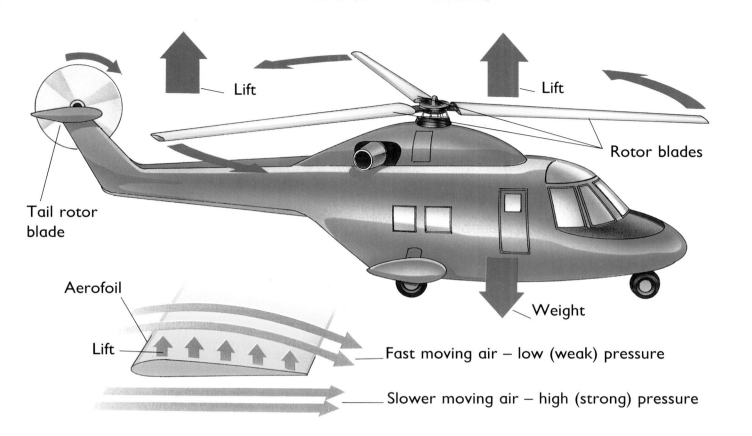

Lift

Lift

Rotor blades

Tail rotor blade

Aerofoil

Lift

Weight

Fast moving air – low (weak) pressure

Slower moving air – high (strong) pressure

▲ An aerofoil is the curved surface of a rotor blade. As an aerofoil travels through the air, the air flowing over the curved surface is faster than the air travelling under it. This means that the fast moving air creates lower (weaker) air pressure above the aerofoil than the slower moving air under it. So, the aerofoil creates 'lift'.

▲ When the rotor blades spin, air is pushed down past them and the helicopter is pulled upwards. The blades act as aerofoils.

Helicopters can hover in one spot as long as the blades spin and air is pushed downwards. A small rotor blade on the tail stops the main blades from twisting the machine round. It is used to steer the helicopter.

Glossary

air pressure The weight of air that presses down on the earth's surface. Low air pressure is weak, high pressure is strong.

axle A rod that goes through the centre of a wheel. The wheel turns around the axle.

bevel When a surface meets another at an angle. A bevel wheel has teeth cut into an angled, cone-like surface.

bore To make a hole.

dams Structures built to hold back water.

drill bit Metal rods with spiral grooves cut into them. They are fitted on to drills and used to bore holes in hard material, such as wood.

drive wheel The wheel or gear in a machine which passes on energy from the motor.

electric Relating to electricity, which is a form of energy.

energy The power needed for doing something.

force The push or pull needed to move objects, or to change their speed or direction.

gear wheels Wheels with teeth that fit together and turn to change speed or direction.

generator A machine that produces electrical energy.

grindstones The flat circular stones used to grind (break down) grain seeds into flour.

motor A machine which makes something work or move. A motor is worked by energy from electricity or fuel.

paddles Strips of wood in a waterwheel that catch the moving water.

propellers Specially shaped blades, on a shaft or pole, which revolve to drive a ship or aircraft forward.

reel A wide wheel on which lengths of material, such as thread or film, may be wound.

revolves Turning round and round.

sluice A water channel with a gate to let an even flow of water through.

spindle A rod on which a machine turns.

turbines Machines which use the power of moving air, water or steam turning rotor blades round and round to create energy in a generator. Turbines are often used in power stations.

Books to read

First Technology series by
  J. Williams (Wayland, 1993)
Gears (Toy Box series) by
  C. Ollerenshaw & P. Triggs
  (A & C Black, 1991)
Gears, Motors & Engines by
  A. Ward (Watts, 1992)

Helicopters (How it goes series)
  (Watts, 1993)
Machines at Work by A. Ward
  (Watts, 1993)
Starting Technology series by
  J. Williams (Wayland, 1991)

Picture acknowledgements

Art Directors Ltd 6, 24; Cephas 5 (S. Boreham), 19 (E. Burt), 22.(N. Blythe); Eye Ubiquitous 20 (B. Pickering); S. & R. Greenhill 14; Robert Harding 9 (M. F. Chillmaid), 11, 26, 28; Tony Stone Worldwide title page, 16 (T. Garcia), 23 (R. Tully); Wayland Picture Library 4, cover background and inset, 12 – 13 (A. Perris/APM Studios). All artwork is by Peter Bull.

Index